PDQ PRO

Prepare, Develop, and Qualify a Proficient Team

William PARRY

Edward BEALE

William Parry - Edward Beale

Copyright © 2025 William J. Parry & Edward K. Beale
All rights reserved.

No part of this publication may be reproduced, stored in a retrieval system, or transmitted in any way by any means, electronic, mechanical, photocopy, recording, or otherwise without prior permission in writing from the author(s) except as provided by USA copyright law.

PDQ PRO is a work of nonfiction.
www.pdq-pro.com
9 8 7 6 5 4 3 2 1
FIRST EDITION

Book design by Edward K. Beale. Edited by Alison (Downs) Petrowski.

Published in the United States of America.
Library of Congress Control Number: 2025910502
Self-Published by Expeditionaire
East Brookfield, Massachusetts, USA.
Parry, William | Beale, Edward
/ pdq pro: prepare, develop, and qualify a proficient team /
/ William Parry Edward Beale /
1. Nonfiction / Business
2. Nonfiction / Education
11.11.25
ISBN: 0-9976601-1-1
ISBN-13: 978-0-9976601-1-1

PDQ-Pro: Prepare, Develop, and Qualify a Proficient Team

Bringing clarity to front-line managers everywhere

William Parry - Edward Beale

CONTENTS

	Introduction	vii
	Part One – The Big Picture	Pg 1
1	The Challenge	Pg 3
2	The Roadmap	Pg 9
3	Finding the Route	Pg 13
4	PDQ-Pro – an Example	Pg 25
	Part Two – The Process in Depth	Pg 29
5	Step 1: Focus on the Role	Pg 31
6	Step 2: Find the Rock Stars	Pg 37
7	Step 3: Uncover the Ecosystem	Pg 43
8	Step 4: Focus on Activities	Pg 51
9	Step 5: Focus on Knowledge	Pg 57
10	Step 6: Focus on Quality	Pg 65
11	Building the Roadmap	Pg 73
	Part Three – The Next Level	Pg 99
12	Focus on Coaches	Pg 101
13	Pro – Proficiency (and Professionalism)	Pg 109
14	The Secret Sauce	Pg 113
	Notes	Pg 117
	Acknowledgements	Pg 119

INTRODUCTION

We graduated the U. S. Coast Guard Academy, and as new Ensigns were ordered to the Cutter MUNRO. In our new role, *Deck Watch Officer*, we had to learn how to safely navigate a 378' High Endurance Cutter out of San Francisco Bay and into the chilly waters of the Bering Sea, north of Alaska. Driving the ship required extensive knowledge and experience; not only to direct its path, but also to direct the actions of the crew.

If we told you that on the first day, the captain of the ship announced, "take 'er out, she's all yours!" you'd have serious questions about how the Coast Guard did business. No captain in their right mind would turn over a multi-million-dollar ship to a bunch of 20-something year-old new Ensigns!

Before we could drive the ship, we had to *learn* the skills, then *demonstrate* the skills, and finally *prove* our skills – to a cadré of subject matter experts who would put their names on our qualification. They would vouch for our competence: no extra classes or schools, just on-the-job learning, practice, and coaching.

We spent time in every department that would impact getting success as a ship driver. It took many hours each day over several months to get the ins and outs of the ship down perfectly.

Granted this example may seem extreme. Yet, how many times have you seen a new hire get "handed the keys" before they were fully proficient to "drive the ship"? Could they be trusted to do it the right way? Were they competent to represent your brand? Are they really qualified? How do you know?

More important: how can you sleep at night?

Here's the fun little secret. The learning steps needed to drive a ship or deliver results for your team are exactly the same. You can apply these steps to any workplace role, and you can do it without an advanced degree or any special training.

The steps are found in this book.

The solution is effective, inexpensive, and builds team cohesion in the process. The solution is used every day to certify radio operators, fire fighters, mechanics, cooks, deck hands and yes, ship drivers. In the military it's called the Personnel Qualification System.

Here we call it "PDQ-Pro" which is short for

Prepare ⇒ Develop ⇒ Qualify ⇒ PROficiency

The process brings structure to the timeless and well-understood "Master to Apprentice" approach, and integrates adult learning theories in a way that's completely invisible to the new performers. In short, it's perfect for developing new teammates, and you'll be able to know someone is qualified using a measurable qualification process.

By following the basic steps outlined here, you will be able to efficiently amplify the knowledge of your existing high performers, and confidently shorten time to qualification for the new people in your "boat."

Most important: you'll be able to sleep at night.

If you're a busy team leader, overextended manager, or a volunteer coordinator trying to herd cats as you take people new to a role and get them "driving the boat" with proficiency and confidence, this book is for you.

Welcome aboard! Let's get started.

William Parry - Edward Beale

PART ONE

PDQ-PRO - THE BIG PICTURE

This book is for every team leader or manager trying to get results in a fast-paced world. To kick it off, we explain the model, demonstrate the process, and give a simple example of PDQ-Pro in use.

William Parry - Edward Beale

CHAPTER 1

THE CHALLENGE

Today's world has pushed teams into a frenzy of constant growth. We're overwhelmed with shiny apps, buzzwords, fancy metrics, and cries of "just do more". The quest for that one silver bullet has drowned out the basics of human performance.

As we move into a new era of business, emerging companies with young teams will start a rapid growth spurt that will boggle the mind. To manage the growth, organizations will put top performers into manager roles and expect them to duplicate their performance by cloning themselves.

Unfortunately, these top performers are very often lone wolves and only know how to produce results. They aren't necessarily equipped to raise a team of top performers. Often their leadership style is "just do what I did," and they miss the mark on helping a team grow while causing more harm than good.

Even worse is the tendency to become Super Performers who swoop in to close every deal or fix every problem. In short order, you get poor or inconsistent results, a team without qualified performers and low morale, bad leadership skills, and high turnover where tribal knowledge walks out the door and more money gets spent to find and develop new talent.

Then there's classroom training. Classroom training is expensive. When your people go to training, they're not in the field doing the work. Travel, per diem, and lodging add to the cost. Then there's the cost to write instruction, furnish and maintain the classroom, and pay for the instructor. Even if these are sunk costs for a large company, they're still costs. (This is why many teams now use in-class training as a "last step.")

Think back to the last time you were in a classroom that even *tried* to resemble your workplace, and you'll agree – the classroom never perfectly models the real world. Training materials always lag behind workplace changes. You just can't replicate field conditions in the classroom. Plus, the instructional staff probably hasn't been on the front line in a while. As a result, your performers get old information from rusty experts.

We had this challenge, over and over. It was brutal. So, we asked a simple question. "What if we could find a system that would:

- Clearly identify what a team member needs to KNOW or DO in order to succeed; and then
- **Prepare** them with factual and procedural knowledge from the right resources and people;
- **Develop** their skills under expert coaching and supervision; and
- **Qualify** them *quickly*, as they demonstrate competence across a range of skills that *get results*?"

(Obviously it also would be great to have something that creates team synergy and energizes the established employees, and gives leadership some confidence that new hires will be proficient on the job.)

As we mentioned in the introduction, the PDQ-Pro approach is derived from a simple skill development system called "the Personnel Qualification System," used by the U.S. military. PDQ-Pro streamlines the concept so any front-line manager (you) can build a rapid roadmap to help your new associate achieve competence and proficiency.

You want to shorten time to qualification for *all* your new employees. On the job (OTJ) and shadowing can only get you so far. You need structure and coaching that can build knowledge and skill quickly. You need a shortcut to performance.

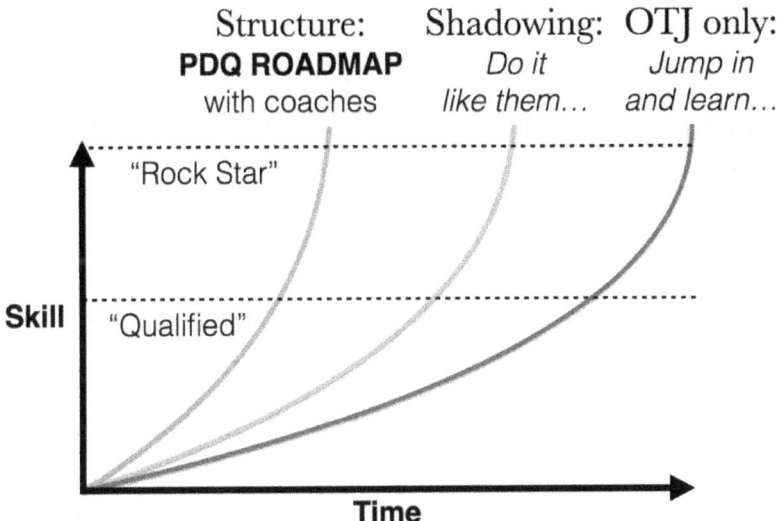

In a nutshell, your trainees follow a **roadmap** as they develop knowledge and skill, then get checked by your best performers who verify competence in the role. You write the roadmap. They work with your team's top performers. The roadmap guides them to a final qualification, and you have a verifiable record of their success.

First, a candidate completes self-study to **Prepare** for supervised practice. This builds responsibility and initiative as the new hire "pulls" from current references used on the job, the key resources that serve as a foundation for performance. This section is focused on *knowledge development* and answers the question, "to get quality results, what do they *NEED TO KNOW?*"

Then, the candidate performs tasks under supervision, to **Develop** skill through repetition and focused coaching. Training and support programs, on-the-job activities, "senior-to-subordinate" instruction, and in-the-field performance are all critical elements. As their manager, you target specific *skill development* based on the question, "to get quality results, what do they *NEED TO DO?*"

Finally, the candidate demonstrates competence across the collective range of skills, as they **Qualify** to perform in the role. Gatekeepers verify the associate can meet performance metrics – that they can get *quality results*.

As their manager, you need to answer the question, "*HOW DO I KNOW* they can perform this role?"

Being able to answer this question helps you sleep at night.

After initial qualification, development continues as they repeat the **Prepare** – **Develop** – **Qualify** cycle with new products, new customers, and advanced tasks, to build *prowess* and maintain **PROficiency**. In short, you guide their continued growth as a *PROfessional*.

THE CHALLENGE - TAKEAWAYS

Qualification is just an empty word if quality performance can't be measured and repeated.

Getting quality performance doesn't need to be hard, it just needs a little structure.

William Parry - Edward Beale

CHAPTER 2

THE ROADMAP

Your organization may not have resources like the military. But like most things, you can start where you are, use what you have, and do what you can.

Each team member needs to KNOW things, DO things, and deliver QUALITY results. A new hire may already have plenty of experience. But they are *new to the role* with your team. They need to understand how *you* expect things done, how *your* organization gets results. They need to crawl first, then walk, then run – and then keep running.

It's your job to get them a map of the road,
                Pretty Darn Quick,
                            so they can perform like a Pro.

The heart of the process is a roadmap. With a roadmap you give a new performer the entire picture of their development – your expectations – in a single overview. Think of it like this: you are handing them directions to get from where they are (unqualified in the role) to where they should be (fully competent and qualified in the role). If they follow the roadmap and hit all the checkpoints, you'll have peace of mind that they covered the entire route and took no short cuts.

Just like every destination needs a different set of directions, each qualification roadmap is role specific. A basic set of skills, something they could learn in a day, needs the simplest roadmap - a single sheet of paper. For more complex roles, the roadmap might be a multi-page document. You could even collect several roadmaps together into a complex qualification guide, or use an online Learning Management System (LMS) to assign and track progress along "the road."

While the length of the roadmap and the tool to track progress can vary, any role requires specific knowledge and skills, performs actions, and makes decisions to get results. The roadmap lines up these "checkpoints" to reach the destination: a final qualification.

As you build the roadmap, you also select the very best of your people (who are already qualified in the role) to act as coaches and guides. For simple roles it could be just one person - maybe you. If the expected performance is complex, your new hire may need to be coached by a whole team. Again, this is role specific.

The process to build a roadmap will always be the same. The first part of each roadmap lists any required or useful "getting started" information. This is the "book knowledge" they'll need. It could be actual books and manuals of course, but also online learning and required training. This is where they *learn from theory*. A new hire might come with most of this already done, but the roadmap is *your* chance to walk through and *verify* how well they know the basics. Here is where they PULL to **Prepare** for the role.

Next, the roadmap lists small tasks and actions that are building towards qualification. Eash task should be something they can demonstrate to you, or to the carefully selected top performers (coaches) on the team. Here they *learn from practice*. With coaching, modeling, and repetition, they DO to **Develop** proficiency.

Finally, the roadmap brings everything together from the prepare and develop sections. You and your top performers will QUERY to **Qualify**, focused on each critical performance that gets results. Some actions and activities may need multiple demonstrations before you can consider the new hire to be fully qualified and **PRO**ficient.

In the next few chapters, we'll help you build a road map. You'll select what a new hire needs to *know* as they Pull to **Prepare**, *demonstrate* as they Do to **Develop**, and the role-specific critical activities to *validate* as you Query to **Qualify**. And we'll help you pick which qualified people would make the best coaches.

KEY TAKEAWAY
The PDQ-Pro roadmap is a simple, structured way to verify and track development in a role.

CHAPTER 3

FINDING THE ROUTE

If you're someone who just reads the "CliffsNotes" short cuts, then this chapter is for you.

Like any set of directions, you need turn-by-turn instructions to get your new performer from where they are now (unqualified) to where they need to be (verifiably qualified). As the manager, it's your game board and you probably have a pretty good idea what pieces you already have, like online courses, reference manuals, seasoned top performers in the role, customers and suppliers, annual goals and metrics, product specifications, and industry requirements.

Now it's time to bring all those things to the surface and out on the table, and line them up for your new person to follow. As a reminder, the roadmap you are building will fill three buckets on the way to final qualification and proficiency in the role:

Prepare ⇒ Develop ⇒ Qualify = PRO

Focus on someone *in a specific role*, then grab a piece of paper and take notes as you go through these six steps:

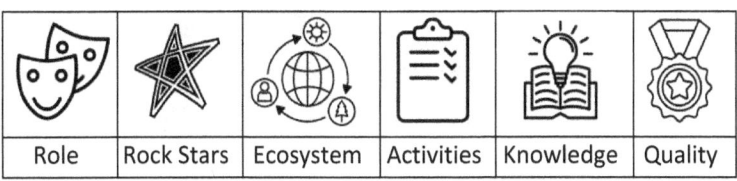

| Role | Rock Stars | Ecosystem | Activities | Knowledge | Quality |

THE ROLE

STEP 1: FOCUS ON THE ROLE (IN DEPTH: *CH. 5*)

First, focus on the role and ask, "what does this person need to KNOW and DO to GET RESULTS in this role?" Complex roles may need 30 days or more to be productive. Other roles need to be productive in days, hours, or minutes. Ask yourself, "if this person had to cover the role for a week, what is the bare minimum they would need to KNOW and DO so I could sleep at night?"

- "Why do we have this role?" (obviously to generate results, but be specific – why is this role "in house"? Why not outsource?)
- "What is a person in this role supposed to do every day?" (Keep in mind, it may not be what someone in that role is actually doing.)
- "I need to see a new hire doing *this* in the first day/week/month." Write down three activities that generate good performance, that are vital to success

in the role. Keep going to capture 15 or 20 actions that yield high quality results.

- "If someone new to this role could do just ONE thing perfectly at the end of the first week, what would it be?"

THE ROCK STARS
(Subject Matter Experts)

STEP 2: FIND THE ROCK STARS (IN DEPTH: *CH. 6*)

After a first look at the role itself, you'll probably realize somebody on your team is already performing at a high level in that role. That person is your Rock Star performer.

We sometimes call them the Subject Matter Experts (SMEs). They know all the answers, they have all the keys, they know where the ~~bodies~~ secrets are kept, and who to talk to, in order to really get results. You need to find these people, pick their brains, and involve them in the process.

Your goal when scrutinizing the Rock Stars is to capture what works for your top performers in the field. They know the shortcuts to performance. They've made the mistakes and found ways to fix them, they've hit all the road blocks and found ways around them, and they've seen it all and lived to tell the tale.

Have a conversation with these top performers. Have *them* tell *you* what the new hire needs to KNOW and DO to get results in the role!

THE ECOSYSTEM

STEP 3: UNCOVER THE ECOSYSTEM (SEE: *CH. 7*)

A tree in the jungle doesn't grow alone, but is part of a wider ecosystem. In the same way, there is a performance ecosystem surrounding each role. Equipment, suppliers, software systems, and coworkers all contribute to this person getting results – their ecosystem of support. A good roadmap will introduce a new hire to the critical touchpoints and people as they work towards qualification.

Look *inward* to company resources and processes that impact the role. Look *outward* – key customers, competitors, critical suppliers, or government regulators. Think about *time* – the product cycle, perishible components, key deadlines, and seasonality.

ACTIVITIES

STEP 4: FOCUS ON ACTIVITIES (IN DEPTH: *CH. 8*)

Make a list of the productive activities *in the role* that get results. Cut it down to the 10 or 15 actions that have the most impact. Consult your Rock Stars to identify and narrow the list. Don't cut too much! You need to give the new performer a *simple* but *complete* road map to become proficient in the role.

- To get high-quality results, what do they need to DO?

- What on-the-job actions and activities define the role?

KNOWLEDGE

STEP 5: FOCUS ON KNOWLEDGE (IN DEPTH: *CH. 9*)

All jobs have a knowledge component. It's background stuff you need to know, or know how to find, in order to be successful. This includes regulations, information in a database, product specifications and instructions, e-learning modules, even online videos or podcasts. (These are just a few of the many options someone new to the role can use to find or locate the knowledge required to get results.)

Your job as their new manager or team lead is to get them up to speed quickly. You are curating and pre-sorting all the possible sources and narrowing it down to the critical few references or bits of knowledge.

Take a few minutes and focus on what the person **NEEDS TO KNOW**. We call all this the "Pull to Prepare" stuff. Remember, once the new performer is qualified they may or may not have you or anyone else to ask for an answer. They will (almost certainly) need to PULL the answer themselves. It helps if you've already walked them through (using a PDQ-Pro roadmap) where to find answers to all the regular issues, the contingency problems, and of course any emergencies associated with the role. At any time they may unexpectedly be called upon to save the day, so make sure they have all the tools before that happens!

Here are a few more questions to answer in your hunt for knowledge items to include on the roadmap:

- What manuals are needed on the job?
- What regulations and policies are critical in the role?
- What written job aids do top performers use?
- What formal learning is required? Prerequisite classes? Online training? Certificates?
- Any informal learning that supports success? Podcasts? Videos? Websites? Wiki or Knowledge Base (KB)?
- What must absolutely be committed to memory? How perfect must they be, or will they have time to look things up? Where should they go to look it up?

QUALITY

STEP 6: FOCUS ON QUALITY   (IN DEPTH: *CH. 10*)

The final step is where you define what "good" looks like. Ask, "how do I *know* this person is qualified?" Quizzes, verbal checks, timed tests, demonstrations, and role plays can all help *measure quality* and give piece of mind that they are qualified to get results.

- What does *good* performance look like? What does *bad* performance look like? What are the standards? How do you know?
- List any established metrics, dashboard gauges, milestones, award levels, customer feedback targets – anything the associate uses as a performance benchmark.
- This can be as simple as the "go / no-go" criteria for the role, a gut-check of their proficiency.
- At the end of their development roadmap, can you sign them off as qualified and sleep at night?

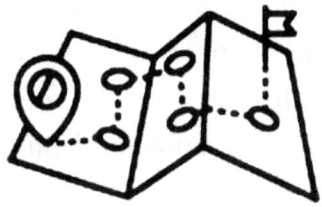

THE ROADMAP

Great work; you're almost done! Now it's time to build the roadmap for someone new to the role.

Go back over your notes and start filling in the three parts of a role-specific developmental road map:

The **Prepare** section is where to list the required prerequisites and certifications for the role – essentially the "book knowledge" needed to get results. Sources could be manuals, e-learning, mandatory training modules, and local references. For example, a new cook must master food-safe hygiene rules and know where to look up recipes before they ever step into a kitchen.

The **Develop** section is where to list all the small daily activities the person needs to do on the job to get results. These are parts of the whole. Using the "new cook" example, they must learn to chop food and safely operate the oven before they are qualified to prepare a meal.

The **Qualify** section is where the person demonstrates to a coach their overall competence in the role. Deciding what passes for competence will depend on many factors: simple jobs will be easier to qualify, complex jobs will have more requirements: training a line cook is easier than developing a head chef.

Now that each section on the roadmap is filled out, take some time to organize and put the milestones in order. Some things need to be completed first because the person will need them later, and some things can be learned at any time. Remember that you're building a road map, so try to string the performance requirements of each section in a logical order.

This is definitely a back-and-forth process. As you populate the road map, you'll discover critical development items you left out, or items that are not really required for success in the role. (It's OK to create the first version of a roadmap, try it out, and adjust it as you continue to develop more new teammates.)

You should also have your Rock Star performers validate the roadmap. They can fill in any vital but missing knowledge and skill development items.

The final step is to draft an ordered checklist, a cookbook or *roadmap* for the new person to follow. Each knowledge item or skillset will include a signature block where someone already qualified in the role will observe and approve the new person's performance.

The roadmap can be simple: one or two pieces of paper. Other roles might require a more complex and longer roadmap, or you might bundle several roadmaps together into a final qualification. An example might be a new sales associate who needs three roadmaps to qualify for the role: one to demonstrate product knowledge, another for customer knowledge, and a third to demonstrate sales techniques.

Keep in mind that it is often expected and sometimes easier to substitute a digital tracking system for paper. But the development and qualification items you include on the roadmap will be the same.

The next graphic is a summary of what should go into a good PDQ-Pro roadmap. As we've said before, everything you build should be role-specific for someone new to the role, and can also be validated by top performers already on the job.

PDQ-Pro Roadmap Overview

P	**Prepare** *Fundamentals Book Knowledge The Basics*	Definitions and role-specific terminology References, both written and electronic Procedures, including normal and emergency Role-specific pre-certifications and training
D	**Develop** *Small Actions and Tasks Decision-making*	Sub-tasks of more complicated activities Develop habits and speed Maintain safe practices Build efficiency and judgement
Q	**Qualify** *Verification of Competence in the Role*	Put it all together for "the final" Demonstrate integrated knowledge and skill Complete technical exams and sign-offs Pass oral & practical checks for Final Qualification
Pro	**Proficiency**	Practice, practice, practice Stay up to date with what's new Become a coach for others

The next chapter will walk you through a simple example, as we build a typical PDQ-Pro roadmap from start to finish.

FINDING THE ROUTE - TAKEAWAY

Define role expectations based on Rock Star performance. Then develop a great roadmap to Prepare, Develop, and Qualify someone new to the role.

CHAPTER 4

PDQ-PRO – AN EXAMPLE

If you've read this far you have everything you need to build a great road map and get your new people started, PDQ. This is a quick and dirty example of how someone like you might apply the steps from Chapter 3 to create a roadmap for new associates.

We start with a fictitious company that makes gizmos and widgets, the ever popular "*Gizmets, Inc.*"

Gizmets, Inc. is growing fast and hires a new sales associate, Pat. Pat's manager opens this book to Chapter 3, and does a quick 6-step analysis:

1. **ROLE**: To be successful, a good *Gizmets*™ seller must follow the prospecting script, qualify a new customer using the standard flow chart, submit new orders without error, and follow up a sale within 14 days. Every new hire must be getting results by the end of their first month on the job.
2. **ROCK STARS**: Kai and Robin broke *Gizmets*™ sales records last year. They'll oversee the development roadmap and be coaches for Pat.
3. **THE ECOSYSTEM**: A quirky customer in Pat's area requires a secret handshake before any new sale.

Also, local regulations require adding specific language to any new contract.

4. **ACTIVITIES**: Cold calling, order entry, contract generation, and the secret handshake are all critical to Pat's success.
5. **KNOWLEDGE**: Pat needs to use the *Gizmets, Inc.* prospecting guide, and adhere to all local regulations.
6. **QUALITY**: The sales flow chart is essential for tracking metrics. The secret handshake is critical to keeping a key customer. Timely follow-up is a hallmark of the brand. Most tasks must be completed at least three times to achieve mastery.

Using all this information, Pat's manager creates a development qualification card or "roadmap":

Phase	Tasks and Activities	Passed by	Date
	Gizmets, Inc - Roadmap for Junior Sales Associate: PAT		
Prepare	- Pass regulations training online - Pass prospecting written test	*Kai* *Robin*	*2-Apr* *3-Apr*
Develop	- Demo cold calling (3x) - Demo prospecting script (3x) - Demo new order submission (3x) - Demo customer follow-up (3x) - Demo secret handshake (5x)	*Kai* *Robin* *Robin* *Kai* *Robin*	*6-Apr* *8-Apr* *9-Apr* *20-Apr* *10-Apr*
Qualify	- Prospect, qualify, and place a new customer order using the flow chart, with no errors (3x) - Follow up to close an order (3x)	*Robin* *Kai*	*22-Apr* *15-May*
	Gizmets, Inc. Qualified: Junior Sales Associate *J. M. D. Manager*		*16-May*

With roadmap in hand, Pat starts with online training, then completes hands-on tasks to earn coach signatures, and finally aces the qualification "exam". With all tasks complete and verified, the manager signs Pat's final certification as a new Junior Sales Associate.

PDQ-PRO EXAMPLE - TAKEAWAYS
Repetition and expert coaching drive high quality outcomes. Structure and documentation create peace of mind.

William Parry - Edward Beale

PART TWO

THE PROCESS IN DEPTH

In Part One you learned about the PDQ-Pro roadmap, the high-level steps to start building one for your own team, and saw an example of how to follow the steps to create a roadmap for a simple role.

In Part Two, we'll walk you through all six steps as we gather information to build a roadmap for your role. A worksheet at the end of each chapter will help start building your own PDQ-Pro roadmap.

We also present three roadmap examples: a simple role learning to paddle a canoe, a more demanding role on the sales floor, and finally an example of a more complex role involving many skills and relationships.

William Parry - Edward Beale

CHAPTER 5

STEP 1: FOCUS ON THE ROLE

Each role is different, that much is obvious. You hire someone because they come with existing skills and knowledge and show the potential to perform for your team. A role-specific PDQ-Pro roadmap lets you validate any prior knowledge and skill, orient the new hire to *your way* of doing things, and verify their skill against an acceptable quality standard, checked by your own local experts.

By focusing on RESULTS you can cut out a lot of steps trying to define quality performance. Consider this role: canoe paddler. Let's be honest: padding a canoe doesn't require in-depth knowledge of how the canoe was built, the history of canoes, or how to forecast the weather. Sure, those things may be important to the overall canoe operation. But for right now the new performer needs to KNOW and DO a very few things:

parts of the paddle, how to grip it, how to follow the paddle cadence, and paddle or stop paddling in time with the others.

The role you're focused on is probably a bit more complex. But the steps are the same. Just like a canoe paddler, any new hire has role-specific knowledge and skill requirements. The emphasis should be on the 10 – 15 actions that get results, and you can build out the roadmap from there.

The job description is a great place to start, and hopefully what they need to do on the job matches pretty well. It might be as easy as organizing items from the job description into two lists: knowledge (Prepare) and skills (Develop).

Knowledge for the role may be something you tested for through the hiring process, or something they can show with a diploma or certificate. But on-the-job knowledge is also important – where to locate something or which reference to use.

Skills can build from basic through advanced – but you want them to get results pretty darn quick, so narrow down the list. Also consider the best traits of others already performing in the role, because those are shortcuts to high-quality performance for a new performer. The workday cadence and 'what good looks like' are other places to start. Don't hesitate to change or add considerations, since each role is different.

Use the worksheet at the end of this chapter to guide your analysis as you consider all aspects of the role. You need to get them from unqualified to fully qualified, Pretty Darn Quick. The worksheet is not a prescriptive straight jacket but is there to prompt your thinking as you focus on the role.

ROLE FOCUS - TAKEAWAY
Each role has a few critical knowledge items and skills that get rapid results for your team. These are what to put on the PDQ-Pro roadmap.

FOCUS on the ROLE worksheet
- a quick first look at requirements and timelines -

Role: Designation or Title

Existing "Job Description" for the role (if available)

First* Actions or Competencies to get qualified *quickly

-
-
-
-
-
-
-
-

Timeline / Deadline to qualify (hours / days / weeks)

FOCUS on the ROLE worksheet

"The Best Performer" in this Role does these things:

My best qualified performer is: (Name)

Quality: "How do you know they did a good job?"

Roadmap Prep

Role:

Time to Qualify:

Vital knowledge needed:

Vital skills needed:

CHAPTER 6

FIND THE ROCK STARS

In chapter three you were introduced to the Rock Star concept. They're your top performers who have all the answers, know all the secrets, and can get results in the role. Your next task is to identify one or more of them, the "Subject Matter Experts" (SMEs), and document what they KNOW and DO to get such good results. PDQ-Pro is all about streamlining the qualification process, using the best of what you have, into a single road map.

Here are some questions to help you get started:

- Who is my best performer? What makes them the best? Who is the next-best performer in the role?
- When things start going badly, who can I always trust to fix it? What makes me trust them?

- If I had to be gone for a month-long emergency, who would cover for me? Why them? While I was gone, what would that person need to DO? Be specific.
- What does your Rock Star USE to be successful in the role? This could be an electronic tool, a job aid, an external web site, a dog-eared reference manual. These things are all ways to jumpstart the roadmap for your new hire.
- WHO does the Rock Star work with to get results? Sometimes that top-notch performance comes from internal and external networks.

Capturing all this can feel like putting lightning in a bottle! There is really no guaranteed simple way to extract performance goodness from your Rock Stars. Each role is different, and each Rock Star SME is different. If you're lucky, you'll have several to help build the qualification road map. The best way to get them talking is this: sincerely value their expertise and keep them focused on the goal - get the new hire helping to "drive the boat" quickly.

Here are a few more questions to help you document and streamline items for your road map:

- "At the end of the day, how do you know you did good work? What do you look for?"
- "Who do you turn to when things start going badly? Why them?"

- Have them finish this sentence: "The most important thing I do every day is _____."
- Prompt with things like "verify," "watch out for," "ensure that," "complete the...," "follow these steps," etc.
- Ask: "If you had a sudden personal emergency and would be away from work for a month, name just one thing that absolutely *had* to be done to keep things running around here? Now, how about one more?"

ROCK STARS - TAKEAWAYS

Your Rock Stars are the Subject Matter Experts who KNOW and DO things that get results.

Rock Star SMEs are the fastest path to building a quality road map.

Find the ROCK STARS worksheet
- High performers already on the job -

Who is my *best performer* in this role?

These actions and knowledge make them "the best:"

-
-
-
-
-
-
-
-

Who is my *next-best performer* in this role?

These actions and knowledge make them "the best:"

-
-
-
-
-
-
-
-

Find the ROCK STARS worksheet

Who do I trust when things start going badly?

What do they do to make me trust them?

-
-
-
-
-
-

Roadmap Prep

Role:

Best performer's knowledge:

Best performer's actions:

My Subject Matter Experts (SMEs) use these tools and documents:

CHAPTER 7

UNCOVER THE ECOSYSTEM

The health of a jungle depends on an interconnected ecosystem. In many ways, business can be considered a jungle. Every performer is part of a wider ecosystem or network of interconnected team members working together to support the organization's goals. Daily interactions with management, people on other teams, as well as teams working with suppliers, distributors, and customers are all key activities that impact each team member – from sales to operations and the C-Suite to the warehouse.

Let's not forget about software and systems that contribute to success in the role – the "how we do things around here" stuff. Getting your new hire connected to the ecosystem and *doing it fast* is critical. To have any level of scalable success, part of their roadmap must include connecting with those who support them. So, let's "walk in the jungle" and map out the ecosystem.

To create your ecosystem map, start with the people who interact with this role. They need to meet the new hire and vice-versa. On a blank piece of paper or whiteboard, draw a circle for the role at the center. Now, add more circles around the edges, and label each one for every person they interact with. Here's the start of your ecosystem.

Next, consider systems and processes connected to the role. A *system* can literally be a mechanical or computer system, perhaps to take orders, enter customer complaints, or assemble a Gizmet™. A *process* can be step-by-step instructions, a style guide or design document, or a decision tree / flow chart. Systems and processes can be sequential, simultaneous, or build upon each other. Remember the goal of a roadmap is to get your new person qualified and delivering results, Pretty Darn Quick. So, simplify this part of the ecosystem to the few systems and processes that get them out there and moving. You'll tack on more depth of understanding and skill over time.

Now, focus on the workplace itself. Part of bringing an employee from new hire to qualified is getting them familiar and comfortable with "the office" and the equipment required on the job. Put these things on the roadmap! Sometimes a quick walkthrough is enough. Other roles require familiarity with several sites and detailed safety procedures. Use the roadmap to capture the few vital aspects of workplace and equipment so your new performer is comfortable in the role and can perform like a pro.

Finally, there's always a timebound aspect of performance. To get results in the role, a new hire must respect the clock and the calendar, with a sixth sense for the passage of time and its impact on their outputs.

Even more important: task repetition. Just because someone did it perfectly once doesn't mean you can sign them off as qualified! How many times must they demonstrate the skill before you can really sleep at night? On the flip side, don't make them do something so many times they get frustrated. There's a balance as they build skill in the role. The roadmap should include some repetition until they "get it" in the eyes of your coaches.

All these things - people, process, place, and time - surround and support the new hire. And your roadmap should introduce them to the entire ecosystem, as you weave a pathway to qualification. To help identify all this wrap-around support, here are a few more questions to get you started:

- WHO else is involved? Who does this role touch? Who touches them?
- Think inward – up the chain, down, and sideways. Marketing? Finance? Customer Service/Support?

- Think outward — suppliers, auditors, advertisers, buyers.
- WHAT else is involved? Computer systems? Order and product management databases? Special tools? Industry-specific materials? Supply chain?
- What's the impact of TIME?
  Product cycles, critical and industry events, quotas, expiration dates, recurring deadlines, even the weather can all be factors that influence the ecosystem.
- How does the work environment itself contribute to getting (or undermining) quality results?

We can't emphasize this point enough: the PDQ-Pro roadmap should be *crafted to build synergy* between the new hire and the existing ecosystem. This is *not* an 'us versus them' game that thrives on competition and animosity! Completing the roadmap is a cooperative effort. Each item should link a new person and their performance to the rest of the "results machine" you already have in place. It's about exposing the new person to all aspects of what it takes to really make an impact for the team.

Now, using the worksheet at the end of this chapter, go back through what you captured about your performance ecosystem. Think about the few critical people, processes, equipment, locations, and events that will contribute to early, fast results for your new hire. Who should they meet? What and where should they visit? Which systems lead to success? How do they fit in with the regular cadence and flow of activity? Capture what they should KNOW and DO within the ecosystem. These items will be part of the roadmap.

Start sketching out the ecosystem around this role:

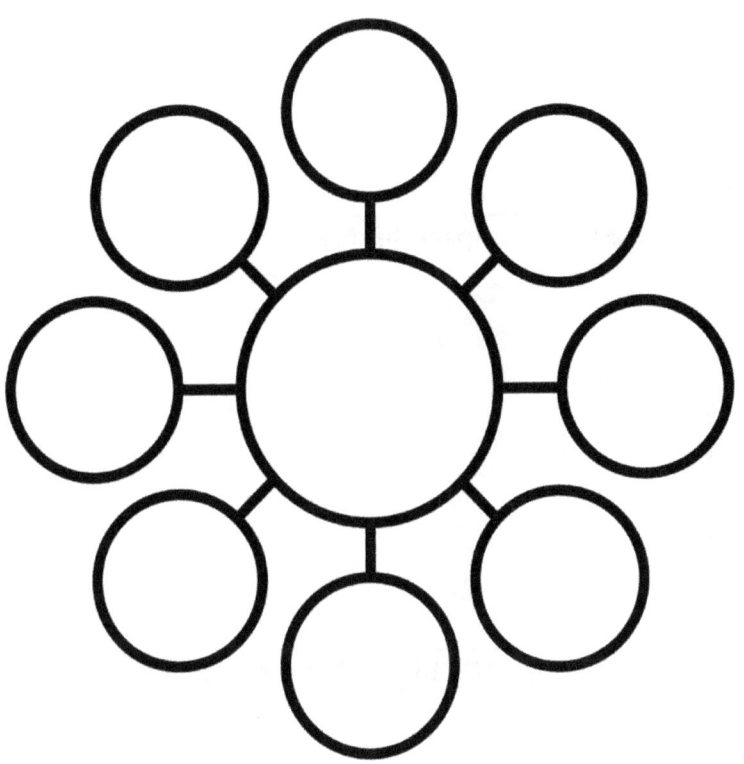

ECOSYSTEM - TAKEAWAY

The performance ecosystem is where building team synergy guarantees fast, quality results.

Uncover the ECOSYSTEM worksheet
- People and Processes that impact success -

PEOPLE who impact this role:

-
-
-
-
-

PROCESSES that impact this role:

-
-
-
-
-
-

EQUIPMENT and TOOLS that impact this role:

-
-
-
-
-

Uncover the ECOSYSTEM worksheet

CALENDAR and CYCLE events that impact this role:

-
-
-
-
-

Roadmap Prep

Role:

Critical People:

Critical Processes:

Critical Equipment and Tools:

Critical Timeframes:

CHAPTER 8

FOCUS ON ACTIVITIES
or *DO to **Develop***

Each team member was hired to perform specific tasks that advance your company's business goals. Without the ability to perform these tasks correctly, they are not ready for the job.

To complete a task, they must DO an activity. Every activity an employee does will bring a result – good, bad or indifferent. The goal is to help your team focus on activities that positively impact your organization's business goals. These are usually increasing profits and decreasing costs, or something unique to your industry. Most likely, it's the one thing that senior leadership is yelling about most often. "We need your team to do more of ... *this!*"

If you can identify that goal, you can focus on the activities that will impact your team's performance the most, and design your learning roadmap around these activities. A tight focus on activities that yield quick results will ensure your team is DOING the behaviors needed to meet your company's critical business goals.

To begin with, ask yourself "what actions get results in this role?" For example, in sales this might be prospecting or closing a deal. In finance it might be budgeting and audits. For construction it might be reading plans and site layout. For hospitality it's a quick guest check-in or reservations management.

Development happens when the trainee watches a task get done, tries a task with help, and does a task by themselves. It is never good enough to just watch a coworker or SME do the task. They must DO it themselves, because eventually they must do the job alone and be accountable for the result. It's why we say "DO to **Develop**."

Again, PDQ-Pro is about getting them through the learning curve pretty darn quick. So, focus on those few things, maybe 5-10 activities, that get them ramped up and producing results in the role. Remember to capture quality for each activity – "what does good look like?"

Answer these key questions to help identify the few critical activities and actions:

- For high-level results, what does this role need to be able to DO and by WHEN?

- What are 5-10 activities they must execute to be worthy of their paycheck?

Capturing a *measurable* action has a format. First you state the CONDITION(S) to start the action. For example, you can't paddle a canoe without a paddle! The paddle is a condition for quality paddling.

Then you state the PERFORMANCE itself – in this case, *paddle* the canoe. Try to use verbs where the new teammate can *show the coaches* a high-quality result. Another way to check verbs is to use the "watch me" test: "Watch me *paddle*" is better than "watch me *understand* how to paddle."

Finally, you list the STANDARD of quality – in this case, paddle in time with the canoe leader and other paddlers.

The worksheet on the next page can help define these critical actions and activities.

ACTIONS FOCUS - TAKEAWAYS

The ability to DO a *few key things well* is the difference between a new hire and someone qualified in the role.

You're paying them for actions that get results.

Focus on ACTIVITIES worksheet
- DO to DEVELOP -

To be successful in the role, what *must* they DO? (top 5)

-
-
-
-
-

What are 5-10 key ACTIVITIES that lead to *success*?

-
-
-
-
-
-
-
-
-
-

Describe one or two HIGH QUALITY *results*:

Focus on ACTIVITIES worksheet

My best performers do these *sub-tasks* to get results:

-
-
-
-

What does a GOOD action *look like*?

-
-
-
-

Roadmap Prep

Role:

Write several conditions / performance / standard statements: (use extra sheets if necessary)

Given __(these conditions)_____ ;

a person in the role will __(DO this "watch me" action)__ ;

with this level of result: __(quality / timeliness)_____ .

Example: With a paddle in a canoe, PADDLE as part of a team, three times, with passing marks by the instructor.

CHAPTER 9

FOCUS ON KNOWLEDGE
or *PULL* to **Prepare**

In response to the rapid-fire questions of a ten-year-old, Bill's exasperated mother would always say "look it up, William!" – great advice that helped build a critical life skill – the ability to answer his own questions. Your PDQ roadmap gets a new hire in the same mindset. They need to "pull" answers on their own. Pulling information will **Prepare** them with knowledge, which is key to getting results in today's world of fast-paced business.

Consider the movie "Cast Away." The hero decides to *sort* his boxes rather than rip them open. This always bothered us - something in a box could be the key to rescue! In survival situations we were taught to "assess the surroundings" and find what's available to get through the day or night, until rescue arrives.

Your job is to open all the boxes and sort the available resources so a new hire can learn the job as fast as possible, so they can go from surviving to thriving. You need to uncover *dense sources of knowledge* as a foundation for learning, those few critical resources – books, manuals, product sheets, shared files, websites – and drive your new hire back to them over and over.

To get started, find any manuals or training programs that are already in place. Ask your team, "What have you been using to bring a new person up to speed?" You'll get some creative answers as you scrub through what you already have and what's already in use. Here's how to narrow down the list:

IT'S ACTUALLY IN USE

Your best performers use these references every day – so ask them. A ragged procedure card kept in a side pocket, an always-open browser tab, a dog-eared reference book, or the company Wiki. If it came from classroom training and got put on a shelf, skip it!

IT'S CURRENT – AND ACCURATE

Anything in print should be a *recent update*, or if it's online, be updated *constantly*. Your best people should say "this [resource] is always right." Identify what they update daily from the field, like a shared folder, OneNote, or pass-down book.

IT APPLIES TO THE ROLE

Find the key resources that help get results *in this role*. It could be specific product information, or a job-aid to process orders or streamline the customer experience.

IT'S ALIGNED WITH PROCESS

A flow chart that guides decisions is better than a table of contents. A simple form is better than going through page after page of web entries.

IT'S PORTABLE – AND QUICK

Your team is probably on-the-go, and references should go with them. Dig in to discover what tools are already in use where the work happens. A searchable database is useless if they can't search it in the field – a printed card may get better and faster results.

TRIBAL KNOWLEDGE

This can be the premiere source of information for a company. Ask around and you'll hear, "Well, what we usually do is..." or, "What we're *supposed* to do or *used* to do was..." Something hidden on an expert's laptop or on a sticky note can be gold for getting results. Capture these informal bits, and include them as part of the **Prepare** roadmap.

Keep in mind, tribal knowledge may be wrong or out of date, so be sure to check it thoroughly before you promulgate anything throughout the company.

When you've found all the written material, and it seems like something is still missing, ask for "the guy." You know, the guy who really knows how to do the job, the guy everyone goes to when they need help. He or she might be your lead subject matter expert and help pinpoint skills and knowledge that a proficient employee uses to get the job done.

Once again, write *measurable* assessments of knowledge using the CONDITION – PERFORMANCE – STANDARD format. This can be tricky for knowledge items, so try to use a "watch me" action verb like *state* or *list* or *write*.

As you did with the actions and activities, use the worksheet on the next page to capture references and knowledge items.

KNOWLEDGE FOCUS - TAKEAWAYS
A roadmap that makes your new hire 'pull' information teaches them 'how to fish'.

Capturing accurate tribal knowledge can yield time-saving short cuts.

Focus on KNOWLEDGE worksheet
- PULL to PREPARE -

The most important reference for this role is:

References and tools *actually in use* for this role:

-
-
-
-
-
-
-
-

Without this database / system, results would suffer:

Some things they need to know *from memory* are:

-
-
-
-
-
-
-

Focus on KNOWLEDGE worksheet

In the field, this role double-checks accuracy by:

Besides formal tools, high performers are really using:

-
-
-
-
-
-
-

Roadmap Prep

Role:

Write several PREPARE section statements using the format: Given (reference) the trainee will (DO this action) with (quality standard).

Example: When asked about a recipe, the new chef will STATE the ingredients from memory with no errors.

"BY WHEN?" How quickly must a new performer be 'fluent' with these knowledge items and references?

William Parry - Edward Beale

CHAPTER 10

FOCUS ON QUALITY or *QUERY* to **Qualify**

Your new associate needs to demonstrate they are qualified to sell your product, they have what it takes to represent your brand, and they can get results on their own with minimal supervision. It's time to get "checked out" and qualify for the role.

You've scrutinized the role from all sides – your expected results and the actions required to get them, what skills and knowledge they need to be successful, and all the wrap-around influences and support impacting their ability and competence. The last things to consider for role development are your standards of quality.

This is where you face the critical question that started this whole journey, the answers that will help you sleep at night: *how do you know* they can do the job?

You've already made a list of knowledge items, skill items, and final actions that are critical for success. Consider each one in order and answer this question:

What does "good" look like?

List any established metrics, dashboard gauges, milestones, award levels, customer feedback targets – anything the associate uses as a performance benchmark. What opportunities should you give the new hire to explain or demonstrate their understanding of the material? These opportunities can range from 'easy and simple' to 'hard and complex':

- Level 1: Quiz - Lowest level and least reliable.
- Level 2: Review Task - Hands on activities that are directly correlated to a performance. (Example: "Show me how to...").
- Level 3: Active Training - Observe the learner in a real-world simulation (role play).
- Level 4: Practical Application - Observe the learner in a real situation using the new skills and knowledge.

Consider this example. To get results in the role, an employee needs to draft and submit a high quality TPS report. What is your standard of "high quality"? How many mistakes are allowed? How quickly should the report be drafted and submitted? Who checks the report before submittal? These standards can all be part of what your Rock Star coach / SME needs to check to approve that item on the road map.

Here are several ways to complete checks on a new performer's abilities:

WRITTEN TEST

This is an obvious check of knowledge. Your earlier work may have identified e-learning or other certifications which are required for the role. Those probably came with a quiz or test built in, so it will be fine to accept a passing score as worthy of a signature on the roadmap.

FIELD TEST

On written tests, we normally try to be objective, but during a field test the examiners can employ some subjectivity. They are judging real world performance in a real-world context. Of course they should assess skill, but they should also evaluate a candidate's decision-making ability and situational judgement. A new performer must be able to roll with the punches during a test scenario, because they'll be making actual calls very soon as a fully qualified performer.

REPETITION

Most people don't get it done perfectly on the first try. It's in your best interest to check their results several times before setting them loose as fully qualified. Also, they might need to complete the tasks multiple times, multiple ways, in multiple locations, or with multiple clients. With repetition we're looking for speed and accuracy. How well does a performer's actions align with standard policy, procedure, and technique? In our TPS example, the new hire would need to draft and submit high quality reports several times before getting the signature.

ROLE PLAY

Everyone hates the practice scenario, but it's one of the best ways to demonstrate proficiency in a complex activity and show good judgment in real time. Consider how many role plays will be enough to get a good feel of their competence. Your Rock Star coaches / SMEs will run through the scenarios, then evaluate proficiency and provide guidance before giving a final signature.

ONGOING SPOT-CHECKS

This is the basis of the message "this call may be recorded for quality assurance and training." Here is where your coaches quiz the new performer as they actually do the job (under instruction). What are your coaches looking for? What does good look like?

RIDE ALONG OR CHECK RIDE

Anyone who has gotten a driver's license completes classroom training, road training, and a final road test, administered by an approved examiner or expert. Follow the same process to complete the roadmap. What should be part of your final "road test" for qualification in the role?

REVIEW BOARD

The quizzes, tests, field checks, repetition, simulation, and on-the-job training are all done. A great way to wrap it all up is an in-person review by a panel or "board". Here you assemble a few of your Rock Star coaches / SMEs – probably the very people who put signatures on the new hire's road map – to sit across the table and check them one last time. This team of experts will probably not even recommend a candidate to sit before them until absolutely sure they are ready.

The Review Board should give challenging scenarios and contingencies, as a check for knowledge, skill, and judgement, not just "stump the chump" with trivia. You want to check how well a candidate integrates their learning with those key actions that get results. This is the "what if scenario" and "walk us through XYZ" stuff.

After you've considered all these quality factors, it might seem too detailed and overwhelming. At the end of the day, you should assess the "gut check" criteria for the role: can they perform everything unassisted; will they embarrass the company; will they endanger themselves or others; and can I sleep at night?

QUALITY FOCUS - TAKEAWAY
Query the new hire to check full competence: knowledge, skill, judgement, and quality.

Focus on QUALITY worksheet
- QUERY to QUALIFY -

At the end of the day, this person must be able to:

-
-
-
-

What can be approved with a quiz?

-
-
-
-

What can be approved with hands-on demonstration?

-
-
-
-

What can be approved with role plays?

-
-
-
-

Focus on QUALITY worksheet

What performances must be approved in the field?

-
-
-
-

Describe what the final qualification checks look like:

Roadmap Prep

Role:

Performances that get results:

What do they need (prerequisites / gear) for success?

How do you know they achieved quality results?

CHAPTER 11

BUILDING THE ROADMAP

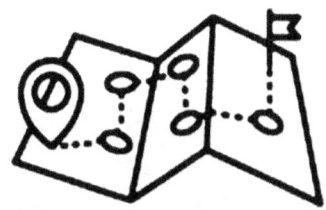

Maybe you skipped directly to this chapter. Good for you! Building a development roadmap is really why you got the book. If you have clarity on what the role must know and do, and what "good" looks like, turning all that into a roadmap should be easy.

Think of it like a syllabus, a checklist, a recipe, or a Merit Badge book. You're writing a set of directions to get someone from where they are now (unqualified in the role) to where they need to be (qualified to perform without supervision). So, let's get started.

The roadmap has three sections:

Prepare: where your trainee "pulls" information as they learn the role, and satisfies their coaches of knowledge;

Develop: where they "do" and repeat key tasks and activities to build skill and judgement that satisfy coaches of their competence;

Qualify: where they demonstrate acceptable mastery of the role as your qualifying coaches "query" them; integrating knowledge, skill, and judgement, with no errors.

PREPARE SECTION

You'd never ask a new driver to jump into the car and drive around – they start in the classroom! In the same way, your roadmap needs to start with the fundamentals. This is where they "learn from theory."

The process to build the **Prepare** section of a roadmap looks like this:

COLLECT ⇒ SIMPLIFY ⇒ SEQUENCE ⇒ CRITERIA

COLLECT

Go back through your worksheets, particularly the one from Chapter 9, and collect up all the required knowledge and prerequisites, and put them together in one place. A good way to do this is on a white board or with sticky notes. Just get ALL the knowledge items, basics, definitions, and references required for the role together in one place.

SIMPLIFY

Now go through the big list and pare it down. Combine similar items or remove something that's already covered by another topic. For example, instead of stating all the parts of a piece of equipment, the roadmap could require stating the five most important parts. Or if a required knowledge item is covered in a prerequisite course, then that course covers both: no need to write "state the parts of the widget" and "complete widget e-learning" if the e-learning course covers all the parts. Do anything you can to simplify the list. This is *rapid* development, remember?

(One last point – you may discover you've listed items that are more involved, beyond just knowledge or reference. Take them off the list, *but save them* for the next **Develop** section.)

SEQUENCE

Now that you have a nice tight list, put the items in order. It's going to make more sense to teach someone *how* to use a database *first*, then *use* the database to find information. Think of this like writing a recipe – you're going to *measure* ingredients before you *mix* them, and mix before you *bake*.

CRITERIA

Each item on your simplified sequenced list needs a pass or fail criteria. They can either state the procedure or they can't. They can use the manual or they can't. They can locate the part number or they can't. Ask, "what's a passing score?" and write it next to each item. Repetition is also important: how many times should they get it right before you're satisfied they have the knowledge? Can just one Rock Star coach approve it, or should several people verify the knowledge? Some items will have easy, cut-and-dried criteria. Other items could be more involved. Your learner has to pass each item on the roadmap, each a steppingstone towards the destination.

Now all that's left to do is transfer your **Prepare** items to the roadmap. Simple jobs can have a single-sheet roadmap, like the one shown for a Canoe Paddler later in the book. Other jobs are much more involved and can have development roadmaps many pages long. We suggest you start with a short, high-level roadmap and add more detail if you discover something missing.

As you write each **Prepare** item or activity on the roadmap, try to give it a measurable action verb. Verifying that someone knows a definition is easier if they SAY the definition or WRITE the definition: you can hear or see the correct answer! We like to call this the "watch me" verb. Don't try to overthink it, but try to make all your **Prepare** items clear and measurable.

Here are some examples:

- DEFINE five parts of the paddle.
- STATE the company's core values.
- NAME the members of the executive management team.
- EXPLAIN the differences between excused and unexcused absence.
- SHOW where to find product specifications in the sales manual.

DEVELOP SECTION

Knowledge can only get you so far. Going back to the driver's license example, your "new driver" passed the classroom portion, but you can't give them a license yet! Now it's time to **Develop** the skills and sub-skills required for competence in the role. This is where they "learn from practice." And, no surprise, you use the same process to build this section of the road map:

COLLECT ⇒ SIMPLIFY ⇒ SEQUENCE ⇒ CRITERIA

COLLECT

Get that big list of activities, actions, and skills together, especially those you uncovered in Chapter 8.

These are things that they DO on the job to get results. Don't go too far down in the weeds with this. Sure, they need to turn a knob or flip a switch, but that's part of a bigger activity or process. Think macro, not micro. Try to find critical things that can be *shown* or *done* to achieve mastery of the role.

SIMPLIFY

Go through the big list and try to "roll up" any smaller skills into a bigger skill. From the driver training example, important sub-tasks are *"put foot on brake"* and *"put key into ignition."* But the skill you really want is *"start the car,"* which incorporates these sub-skills. Use measurable "watch me" action verbs to tighten up the list of activities that get results.

SEQUENCE

Here is where you put yourself in the learner's shoes as they "crawl, walk, run" their way to qualification. Basic skills contribute to more complex actions, so put them first. Safety should be part of this section too – the new driver must click the seatbelt and check their mirrors before putting the car in gear. This is the recipe for development. In the military we say, "train like you fight." So, integrate items from the ecosystem checklist: if your performer has to work with a key supplier in the field, make that part of the developmental roadmap.

CRITERIA

Here again is the "how do you know?" discussion. Skills are typically not learned instantly, a "one and done." Your new hire will need to perform several times, across several days or sessions, and with several different Rock Star coaches before you can be confident they have it down, so you can sleep at night. Think about what good looks like, and how many times it takes to demonstrate basic qualification for a skill.

You guessed it – it's time to transfer all those skill-building statements to the roadmap! Build a good sequence of crawl, walk, run. Include repetition and quality statements. Run the draft roadmap by your Rock Stars as a check – they'll find duplication or stuff that's missing. And phrase each **Develop** item with a measurable "watch me" verb. Here are some examples:

- ENTER a parts order with no errors.
- CONDUCT a price inquiry 10 times.
- CHARGE the credit card on file in less than 30 seconds.
- LOAD a delivery truck with today's orders.
- MAKE a medium hot macchiato with soy milk.

QUALIFY SECTION

By now you should have a good feel for what goes into the road map. Many roles are just a collection of isolated **Prepare** and **Develop** activities, and once all items are signed off the person is qualified for the role. Some roles require the new hire to perform integrated tasks under pressure and high risk, time after time. This is where they "learn from mistakes." The **Qualify** section of the roadmap lays out the final requirements to receive qualification - the big picture, macro view.

At the end of the day, how do you know the person can get results in the role, without hurting themselves or others, and without harming your brand? There's probably a breaking-in period, where the person has shown knowledge and skill but needs more time to get smooth. Driving a car is not about parking one day and braking the next – you need to put it all together every time you go for a drive.

So, include a few summary milestones on the roadmap. Here are some examples:

- MANAGE the hotel check-in desk (under instruction) for three shifts.
- COMPLETE 100 orders with 99% efficiency.

- RUN the maintenance ticket assignments (under instruction) for a week
- RESPOND to a customer complaint with no errors.
- ORGANIZE three client events as the team lead.

FINAL QUALIFICATION SECTION

Any successful course needs a graduation. Every graduate needs a nice piece of paper showing their accomplishment. Be sure your new hire knows they're done! This is the Merit Badge, the completed passport, the golden ticket, the diploma. For someone new to the role, it's a big deal.

Getting that final sign-off and having a small ceremony lets them know you trust them to do the job. It means they followed the roadmap from start to finish and can get results for the team in this new role.

BIG PICTURE REMINDERS

Any roll-out will expose problems with your perfectly developed plan, so expect them. A key advantage of a PDQ roadmap over a "standard" new-hire development program is flexibility, so keep things flexible. Here are a couple ways PDQ-Pro can help structure and standardize rapid performance improvement with a lot less pain.

Use the roadmap with one or two new hires. Tell them they are the test subjects and ask them to help "break" the program. Their job is to validate what is there, identify what works and what needs work, and find things that are still missing.

Keep pulling things back to the macro level. The roadmap needs to incorporate the higher-level process and systems pieces, not all the minutiae. Your coaches are there to get the details right.

Keep things generic in the road map, and equipment changes will not matter. It is better to have someone "update the *customer relationship* database ten times" than it is to "update the *SalesForce* database ten times." Focus on the SKILL, not the GEAR.

The next few pages have actual road maps we have used. Use them as suggestions to help build your own roadmaps. We're sure yours will be much better!

ROADMAP EXAMPLE: CANOE PADDLER

This is a classic PDQ-Pro roadmap on a single page, to qualify a new canoe paddler:

PDQ-Pro for: Canoe Paddler

Prepare

Knowledge and Basics

Fundamentals & Knowledge Activity — Date / Score / Initials

101. Define five parts of the paddle. (with two coaches)
102. Define four sides of the canoe. (with two coaches)
103. State the paddling "prep" command. (with two coaches)
104. Complete Paddler eLearning Course. (90% to pass)

Develop

Skills and Cross-training

Tasks & Processes Activity — Date / Score / Initials

201. Demonstrate paddle grip, both left and right side. (with two coaches)
202. Demonstrate paddling in time to coxswain directions. (with two coaches)
203. Shadow a qualified paddler. (three instances)
204. Shadow a qualified coxswain. (one instance)

Qualify

Coaching and Demonstrations

Performance Activity — Date / Score / Initials

301. Prepare for a canoe paddling excursion. (with two coaches)
302. Put on paddling floatation gear. (with two coaches)
303. Act as a member of a canoe paddling team (three instances)
304. Act as a coxswain for a canoe paddling team (one instance)

Pro

Qualified Canoe Paddler

Qualification Activity — Date / Score / Initials

401. Pass Canoe Paddler *practical* exam.
402. Pass Canoe Paddler *oral* exam.

To take this example a little bit further, here is an even shorter version of the roadmap:

Roadmap for: <u>Canoe Paddler</u>

Prepare: Knowledge and Basics
Date / Score / Initials
Fundamentals Activity
Define five parts of the paddle.   (with two coaches)   ___/___/___
State the paddling "prep" command.   (with two coaches)   ___/___/___
___/___/___

Develop: Skills and Cross-training
Date / Score / Initials
Process Activity
Demonstrate paddle grip, both left and right side.   (with two coaches)   ___/___/___
Demonstrate paddling in time to coxswain directions.   (with two coaches)   ___/___/___
___/___/___

Qualify: Coaching and Demonstrations
Date / Score / Initials
Performance Activity
Prepare for a canoe paddling excursion.   (with two coaches)   ___/___/___
Act as a member of a canoe paddling team   (one instance)   ___/___/___

Qualified Canoe Paddler
Signature: _____ Date: _____

Compare the original roadmap to this one, and notice which knowledge and skill items are changed or removed. A simplified roadmap is appropriate for someone who comes to the role with some experience. Or you might need to qualify volunteers for emergency response, and the abbreviated qualification card is just enough to get them paddling, Pretty Darn Quick.

ROADMAP EXAMPLE: RETAIL SALES

This roadmap does not explicitly list the three sections for Prepare – Develop – Qualify, (the Knowledge, Skills, and Qualification). However, the steps are all still there, just mixed throughout the pages. It's OK to make the roadmap match your company's requirements and style. Remember the goal: a roadmap that gets the new person on the job and delivering results Pretty Darn Quick.

Wirewize LIVE Qualification Process

Wirewize LIVE is now launching in our stores.

This workbook will help you through the Wirewize LIVE certification. There are three parts to this document.

Part I: Tasks

All tasks must be completed by memory and observed by a manager. You may have more than one manager sign off on the various tasks. Once you have completed the tasks move on to the next section.

Part II: Test

This test must be completed with a minimum passing score of 80. You may use any resources to answer the questions.

Part III: Signature Sheet

After all tasks and testing are completed, have your manager sign and date to confirm that you have successfully completed the certification. Ensure that your full name is included on this page.

When all parts of the Wirewize LIVE certification are finished, fax the last 3 pages to the following number: (555) 666-7777

RESOURCES:

1) Wirewize LIVE Job Aid
2) Wirewize LIVE 8 1/2 X 11 Acrylic Filler
3) Wirewize LIVE SKU cards

William Parry - Edward Beale

TASKS: Complete all 10 tasks from memory.		
Task	Date Completed	Manager's Signature
1. List three (3) benefits of Wirewize LIVE to the customer.	_____	_____
2. List three (3) benefits of Wirewize LIVE to Gizmets, Inc.	_____	_____
3. How do you generate an activation code for Wirewize LIVE?	_____	_____
4. What Wizewords would you use to overcome the objection, "I'm going to do it myself."?	_____	_____
5. What Wizewords would you use to overcome the objection, "It's not worth the added expense."?	_____	_____
6. State two common objections to Wirewize LIVE and what Wizewords you would use to overcome them.	_____	_____
7. How is Wirewize LIVE different than a regular manufacturer's technical support?	_____	_____
8. Explain how Wirewize LIVE mult-brand support can help the customer with complex set up.	_____	_____
9. Explain how Wirewize LIVE complements firedog.	_____	_____
10. Demonstrate your knowledge of Wirewize LIVE by selling any 1 SKU.	_____	_____

PDQ-Pro: Prepare, Develop, and Qualify a Proficient Team

TEST: Complete the following test.

TEST: Answer the following questions. You may use any job aids from Wirewize LIVE. You must answer 8 out of 10 to qualify.

1. Handling a customer service call on the sales floor is a good use of time?
   a. True
   b. False
2. Where would you rather put your time and effort?
   a. A frustrated customer
   b. A busy sales floor
   c. Restocking returns
3. Wirewize LIVE can be sold with firedog?
   a. True or
   b. False
4. Selling Wirewize LIVE is bad for your HTI numbers?
   a. True or
   b. False
5. A one year Wirewize LIVE package costs:
   a. $69.99
   b. $39.99
   c. $99.99
   d. $119.99
6. Customer service for Wirewize LIVE is available:
   a. Monday - Friday
   b. 9am – 5pm
   c. Only on the weekends
   d. 24 hrs a day 365 days a year
7. A Wirewize LIVE Setup Coach can help a customer get the best experience out of their system?
   a. True
   b. False
8. Wirewize LIVE can only help with the following brands:
   a. Toshiba
   b. Panasonic & Samsung
   c. Denon
   d. All Brands
9. To obtain an Activation Code for Wirewize LIVE you need the following:
   a. An employee ID
   b. Enter the ticket number
   c. Select the Wirewize package
   d. All of the above
10. Wirewize LIVE benefits your customer by
    a. Providing a personal setup coach
    b. Helping solve technical problems with a quick phone call
    c. Storing all their component information on line
    d. All of the above

William Parry - Edward Beale

SIGNATURE PAGE: All sections must be signed and dated

	DATE	Manager's Signature
1. Completion of test		SCORE:
2. Completion of tasks		

Name of Sales Associate   Store Number

HE Manager's Name   Signature   Date

When completed Fax the following pages to: 555-666-7777

1) Task Page
2) Test Page
3) Signature Page

ROADMAP EXAMPLE: NEW HIRE ONBOARDING

This example from Gizmets, Inc. is much more complex, covering several phases across 90 days of development. We include it here to demonstrate the flexibility of **PDQ-Pro**, as it scales to a multi-week and multi-system onboarding process.

☐ ▮▮▮▮▮▮▮▮▮▮▮▮▮▮▮▮▮▮▮▮▮▮▮▮▮▮▮ **New Hire Onboarding**

New Hire Onboarding

• •

Overview of the new hire onboarding program.

Gizmets, Inc.

New Hire Onboarding

Overview

Program Goal
The new hire onboarding program will give each newbie the skills and knowledge needed to be a productive member of the team.

A productive member of the team is someone who:
- Daily completes all KPI's
- Consistently meets or exceeds quota.

All instruction is focused clearly on what the iSAMs need to be able to perform to successfully do the job.

Roles
There are four primary players in this onboarding process and they are:

- The New Hire
- Sales Enablement Guide
- Peer Coach
- Area Sales Director

Delivery Methods
The onboarding program is designed to be self-paced and delivered using a combination of several methods. The primary location for much of the content will be created in Brainshark and found in the new hire's Salesforce (SFDC) account under "Brainshark Learning." This will give easy access to the material as the iSAM will spend a large portion of time in SFDC.

Additional content will be delivered as follows:
- Self-paced reading
- Facilitated on the job training (OJT)
- Individual coaching
- Instructor Led Training (ILT)

PDQ-Pro: Prepare, Develop, and Qualify a Proficient Team

New Hire Onboarding

Learning Tracks

The training is broken down into four learning tracks with each track having several modules to support the learning.

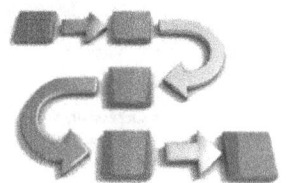

All instruction is focused clearly on what the newbie needs to be able to perform to successfully do the job.

The learning tracks are:

- **Track 1**: *Gizmets and the Industry We Serve*
    - Designed to provide you with a complete understanding of Gizmets as a company and our contribution to the industry we serve.

- **Track 2**: *Systems*
    - After completion of this learning track you will be able to efficiently and correctly use all systems required to perform their job.
    -

- **Track 3**: *Sales Enablement Methodology*
    - Designed to give new hires the ability to consistently execute all sales KPI's daily and meet or exceed quota within two quarters.

- **Track 4**: *Product Knowledge*
    - This learning track gives the new hire the ability to clearly describe the top 3 features and the benefits each product family provides to a client.

New Hire Onboarding

Confirmation of Learning - Testing

Testing is a natural parting of learning. It helps both learners and trainers confirm if the new hire can DO the job competently or identify where something is missing and more action is needed.

All instruction is focused clearly on what you need to be able to perform to successfully do the job.

The levels of testing are:

- **Level 1**: *General Quizzes in Brainshark*
  - A brief quiz will give a general assessment of the learner's comprehension, but it doesn't change behavior. These will be simple checkpoints for a learner's progress.

- **Level 2**: *Review Tasks*
  - **Review Tasks** are hands on activities that require the learner to demonstrate their mastery of the knowledge. Each activity is directly correlated to a performance that impacts sales. Success here is an indicator of strong comprehension.
  - For example, within each training module there will be a series of questions presented that give the learner an opportunity to explain or demonstrate their understanding of the content to one of their guides. It may look like this:
    - "Explain what a Customer Information Form (CIF) is and when it must be executed."
    - "What are the criteria for processing a signed contract for counter signature?"
    - "Demonstrate how to convert a contact to a lead in Salesforce."
  - Once you have demonstrated or explained each task correctly to his/her coach they can then move on to the next level of learning.

- **Level 3**: Active Training (*Role Play*)
  - Active training promotes learning by doing. This experiential learning not only enhances the understanding of concepts but also helps you develop the skills needed to succeed under the direction of a seasoned coach.
  - This "testing" of the new hire's skill set provides an immediate and accurate understanding of the iSAM's comprehension of the material. From this point the guides can confirm their mastery of the skill or reassess for further training.

- **Level 4**: *Practical Application*
  - Observing the new hire in a real-life situation using the new skills and knowledge. Once the new hire has completed a given level of training, they should be observed with live interaction with customers to give a final confirmation of their learning.

PDQ-Pro: Prepare, Develop, and Qualify a Proficient Team

New Hire Onboarding

Professionally Guided

Although the onboarding is "self-paced" the new hire will have a series of guides that direct and coach the learner through the program.

Too often a new hire will get lost, lose interest or be distracted by unnecessary tasks and these guides will help keep the newbie on target and tracking towards completing the program within 90 days.

The first guide will be the **Sales Enablement Guide** who will introduce the learner to the program, show them the path and connect them with the right people to help the onboarding.

The second guide will be the **Peer Coach** who is a subject matter expert in much of the content covered during the onboarding. Most likely this will be a local senior associate who has shown their competence with the material and a willingness to coach.

NOTE: This is an excellent opportunity for someone who is looking to advance their career as it allows them to coach a new hire under the direction of their ASD and the Sales Enablement Guide.

The final guide is their **Area Sales Director (ASD)** who will work with the Peer Coach and Sales Enablement team to provide direction as needed. The ASD has the ultimate responsibility for the new hires overall performance and by working with the other guides, the ASD can maximize your training and still attend to their other managerial duties.

William Parry - Edward Beale

New Hire Onboarding

Track 1: Gizmets and the Industry We Serve

Learning Objectives: After completion of this learning track a new hire will be able to:

- Explain what Gizmets does and clearly describe the industry we serve.
- Locate all resources needed to properly perform their job.
- Direct a client or prospect to any marketing collateral or resource for any Gizmets product family.

Training Modules

1. Module: Gizmets Resources
2. Module: Transformation of Process Engineering – Innovations and Best Practices (White Paper)
3. Module: The Industry We Serve – A General overview of the industry Gizmets serves.
4. Module: The Company Called Gizmets – The Gizmets Story
    a. Welcome To Gizmets
    b. Gizmets - Technology That Loves Complexity
    c. A Culture of Innovation
    d. Operational Excellence
5. Module: Why Safety is Priority One

Track 2: Systems

Learning Objectives: After completion of this learning track a new hire will be able to efficiently and correctly use all systems required to perform their job.

Training Modules

1. Salesforce.com
2. Deal Model
3. Contracts on Demand
4. SLA Sherlock
5. Customer Intelligence Database
6. Pricing Calculator
7. Brainshark
8. WebEx
9. LinkedIn
10. Outlook
11. Halogen
12. Sales Resource Center

PDQ-Pro: Prepare, Develop, and Qualify a Proficient Team

New Hire Onboarding

Track 3: Sales Enablement Methodology

Learning Objectives: After completion of this learning track a new hire will be able to:

- Consistently execute all sales KPI's daily.
- Meet or exceed quota within two quarters.

Training Modules

1. Introduction to Daily Operating Rhythm and KPI's.
2. The MEDDIC system
3. The Engagement Process
4. Pipeline Management
5. Additional modules to be developed in alignment with new sales process.

Track 4: Product Knowledge

Learning Objectives: After completion of this learning track a new hire will be able to:

- For each product family, clearly describe the top 3 features and the benefits provided to a client.
- Describe the expected value for each persona that would use a product.

NOTE: Product training tied into the campaigns along with sale enablement methodology

Training Modules

1. Engineering
2. Manufacturing and Supply Chain (MSC)
3. GizmetsONE
4. Gizmets HYSYS
5. Sales Campaigns
    a. EDR
    b. Economics
    c. Specialty Chemicals

Learning Tracks Series Description

1. 101 Series – All content needed in first 30 days (Beginner)
2. 201 Series – All content needed for 60 Days (Intermediate)
3. 301 Series – All content needed for 90 days (Producer)

William Parry - Edward Beale

New Hire Onboarding

Phase I [30 Days]

Topic	Module

Gizmets & The Industry

Gizmets Culture
- Gizmets Resources
  - Sales Resource Center
  - Sherlock
  - Lynda.com
  - LinkedIn (Networking)
- The Company Called Gizmets
  a. Welcome To Gizmets
  b. Gizmets - Technology That Loves Complexity
  c. A Culture of Innovation

Gizmets Systems

The Industry
- Transformation of Process Engineering – Innovations and Best Practices (White Paper)
- Operational Excellence
- Why Safety is Priority One

Systems
- Salesforce
- Intro to Deal Model
- LinkedIn (Prospecting)
- Outlook

Gizmets Sales

Sales Enablement
- Modules To Be Developed
- Intro to Operating Rhythm & KPIs
- MEDDIC

Gizmets Products

Products
- Introduction to campaigns
- Overview of all product families

Check Point Confirmation of learning: Quiz? Role Play? Audible Ready? TBD?

PDQ-Pro: Prepare, Develop, and Qualify a Proficient Team

New Hire Onboarding

Phase II [60 Days]

Gizmets Systems

(Will vary depending on UPA or New Logo)

Topic	Module
Systems	➢ Salesforce (Intermediate) ➢ Deal Model ➢ Contracts on Demand ➢ Pricing Calculator ➢ LinkedIn (Prospecting – Advanced)
Gizmes Sales — Sales Enablement	➢ Modules To Be Developed ➢ Operating Rhythm Continued ➢ Engagement Process ➢ MEDDIC Continued

Gizmets Products — Products	➢ Campaign participation
	➢ Product Training
	    ➢ Engineering
	    ➢ Manufacturing and Supply Chain (MSC)
	    ➢ GizmetsONE
	    ➢ Gizmets HYSYS

Check Point Confirmation of learning: Quiz? Role Play? Audible Ready? TBD?

New Hire Onboarding

Phase III [90 Days]

Gizmets Systems

(Will vary depending on UPA or New Logo)

Topic	Module
Systems	➢ Salesforce (Advanced) ➢ Deal Model (Advanced) ➢ Contracts on Demand ➢ Pricing Calculator (Advanced) ➢ LinkedIn (Prospecting – Advanced)
Gizmets Sales Sales Enablement	➢ Modules To Be Developed ➢ Operating Rhythm Continued ➢ Engagement Process ➢ MEDDIC Continued ➢ Pipeline Management

Gizmets Products
Products
	➢ Campaign participation
	➢ Product Training
	   ➢ Engineering
	   ➢ Manufacturing and Supply Chain (MSC)
	   ➢ GizmetsONE
	   ➢ Gizmets HYSYS

NOTE: Advanced requires successful application of the system in a real-world scenario.

Check Point Confirmation of learning: Quiz? Role Play? Audible Ready? TBD?

THE ROADMAP - TAKEAWAY

Simple or complex, a good roadmap includes the critical knowledge, skill, judgment, and quality items that produce high-impact results in the role.

PART THREE

THE NEXT LEVEL

Part Two walked you through six analytical steps that expose knowledge, skill, team integration, and quality items that are required for a comprehensive, role-specific PDQ-Pro roadmap. The worksheets helped you simplify those items as you built a roadmap to guide your new team member on their journey to qualification.

In Part Three we'll discuss the integration of PDQ-Pro to build a culture of detail and quality, and how to locate, engage, and reward the real magic behind making PDQ-Pro a winning system: your coaches.

William Parry - Edward Beale

CHAPTER 12

FOCUS ON COACHES AND QUALIFIERS

Imagine you just got hired at Ferrari, and in the first week you started to implement changes to the assembly line where the Prancing Horse had been precisely manufactured for over 80 years. You made the change because, well, you had a better idea. How long do you think you would last?

Manufacturers of high-quality products don't get that way by chance. They have a clearly defined system and process that each team member follows with passion and commitment. For your organization to scale beyond average you must have a strong group of leaders and coaches, all committed to a system that develops a consistent level of performance that brings the results you want.

Let's pause for a moment and turn to the roadmap you have built for new members of the team. In a sense, this roadmap is a "cart" to carry new associates toward a consistent level of performance. It is a defined process that – if followed consistently – will bring your team up to a level of performance and push you towards the goal.

To do this correctly, you will need a strong team of coaches and qualifiers to ensure that your roadmap is followed accurately, consistently, and with measured results.

Let's define these roles.

Coach: these will most likely be your managers and senior leaders. They are seasoned and familiar with (and able to guide and support new hires on) the journey to meet an expected level of high performance in the role. They will guide learners through the roadmap and check final quality performance before signing their name to the approval.

Qualifier: this may be a new term for you, but these people are critical to this program and your success. This is the person that the head of the company will officially designate – in writing – as THE person who says "yea" or "nay" to a new hire's ability to complete a task to a standard set by the leadership team. This person will have demonstrated the ability to do the task correctly, and also observe, evaluate, and instruct a new hire to meet the defined standards.

The right coaches and qualifiers can make or break your PDQ program. Remember, you're trading formal classroom and lab training (with all the expense and infrastructure that requires) for a structured on-the-job experience. Success depends on how well your experienced performers fill in the gaps, quickly, leveraging your new PDQ-Pro roadmap. Picking the right coaches is critical.

Let's dig in a bit to each of these roles and discuss what to look for.

COACHES

If you're a small shop then you might be wearing all the hats, and will be the coach, qualifier, and also give final approval. But ideally, you already have one or more top performers in a manager role acting as a coach. Today's world of business is quickly turning managers into coaches, and we think this is a very good thing. Coaches play a critical role in the success or failure of almost every business that exists.

These people are most often the front line for your front line. They are the people who are making the organizational processes and systems work. They carry out the mission and make sure that every member of their team does so as well. They should be technical experts, operationally accomplished, and have an empathic ability to relate. This is where you should think "Jedi Master."

Some attributes to look for (or develop):

- desire to coach
- strong communicators
- active listening skills
- delegation

- technical expertise
- passion for the profession
- conflict resolution
- ability to explain things to new people
- flexibility in getting results – they can get things done using several different methods
- not only time management, but self-management

Note: this is not an exhaustive list. You'll probably have more to add or remove.

QUALIFIERS

The qualifier is often the SME for the competency, behavior, or task that is being evaluated. They are the "go-to" person who knows how to do it correctly and are the backbone of consistent and scalable performance. For example, they are the person that everyone goes to for help with a specific application, tool, or process.

These people are also the gold seal for your company's processes or systems. They will be certified – in writing – as the expert and approver of an employee's performance for a specific task, behavior, or level of knowledge.

In addition to the knowledge and skill, they should have a "good bedside manner" in the role of coach. It's OK to select a strict (but fair) qualifier as long as they can coach a new hire around to a quality result. They should have a blend of technical expertise, soft skills, and a level of integrity that will uphold the performance values of the organization.

Keep trust in mind. People trust others that they know, people who have helped them in the past, and people they view as competent. New performers learn to trust their coaches. Coaches trust their apprentices to cover for them. Everybody wins.

Here are some attributes to consider when you select your qualifiers. They should be:
- designated in writing;
- someone who knows what's going on;
- a person who wants to grow into a leadership role;
- an acknowledged expert in a specified area of qualification (SME);
- able to handle the responsibilities of a coach:
  - be up to date with relevant skills and knowledge.
  - be able to adjust to *learners'* style (slow/fast etc.) and help them at *their* speed.
  - understand that consistency is the key to success.
- familiar with all reference materials and be able to guide learners to the correct resources. Knowing where to find the answer is often more important than the answer itself;
- focused on the goal of the program which is to develop qualified performers who can do the job consistently and independently;

- courageous and strong enough to NOT give away their signature, but rather to challenge a learner to go back and learn the material;
- available for signoffs and to assist trainees as needed.

OVERCOMING BARRIERS

Setting up your team with PDQ-Pro is exciting but can also cause concern. Here are a few things to anticipate and how you might address them.

Your coaches resist change.
Focus on the results. New people help generate revenue, positive outcomes, and improve metrics, same as them. The faster the team gets results, everyone wins. It's about continually developing the "talent pipeline," reducing time to sale, generating positive reviews, and connecting with customers.

These established experts worry they'll be replaced.
There's a saying that knowledge is power, and long-time employees might worry about losing some of their pull if they pass it along. Some might get a thrill from being the guru or saving the day. Take advantage of the PDQ-Pro structure, which sets them up as a formal and recognized guru.

Fighting burnout.
Anointing a veteran as a coach is a chance to re-energize them by exposure to "new blood." New hire questions will validate successful procedures and techniques and

reveal things to eliminate or overhaul. The veterans have the personal *and* position power to make changes quickly and effectively, but only if they know about the problems. This approach institutionalizes the "undercover boss" idea, where best practices are identified, or missing pieces are addressed quickly.

Turnover is expensive.
With everyone aligned behind the development roadmap, it's easier to build a synergistic team that is focused more on getting results and less on individual competition that causes people to leave. It's always cheaper to develop, retain, and promote from within. New people will learn by example and see a cadré they will join someday as coaches themselves.

"This is too much overhead. I just want to get to work."
Aside from the fact that jumping in without understanding the work is like putting a moose in a glass factory, PDQ-Pro provides structure. Imagine taking a course where the professor says, "start studying, we'll have a test every couple of weeks," then walks out. With no syllabus, it would never fly. Why should you expect that same approach to work in business? Your team deserves more! The learning structure of PDQ-Pro - the fundamentals, systems, and activities which are vital to success in the open market - is not overhead. It's your secret weapon to leap ahead of the competition.

At the end of the day, coaches and qualifiers are rocket fuel for your up-and-coming Rock Star performers. They point the way, provide a gentle push, confirm the learning, and make PDQ-Pro work for your team.

COACHES AND QUALIFIERS - TAKEAWAYS

The old crew can teach the new crew.

The new crew can re-inspire the old crew.

Rock Star Coaches and Qualifiers *must also have* good "bedside manner."

Learners follow the roadmap,
but Coaches pave the road.

CHAPTER 13

PRO - PROFICIENCY
(AND PROFESSIONALISM)

PDQ-Pro is all about rapid skill building for your team. They've learned just enough to get results in the role, and you can finally sleep at night. But that's not where it stops!

Think back again to getting a driver's license. We always joked about "knowing enough to be dangerous." That same humility should keep your best performers coming back for more – being qualified in the role is just a start. Now they can layer on deeper understanding, build judgement in more scenarios, and expand their reach and impact across the entire performance ecosystem.

Plus, these newly qualified associates are going to be your coaches and qualifiers before very long. In a month or a year, they will lead new hires through the roadmap, and keep adjusting to new equipment, customers, and processes.

After initial qualification, let them feel your trust for a while. Let them do the job – they've earned it. Soon you'll hand them a new PDQ-Pro roadmap to tack on a new skill, like a new driver going back to get a commercial license. You can layer and build skill with each additional roadmap. Here's an example:

Gizmets, Inc. has two Divisions, Gizmos and Widgets, each with a unique PDQ-Pro roadmap for their sales associates. However, the two divisions have a single warehousing operation. To advance to sales manager, a Gizmets sales associate completes a new Warehousing PDQ-Pro roadmap.

It looks like this. The top and bottom Sales roadmaps have PDQ development "buckets" leading to a Sales diploma. By completing the common Warehousing roadmap, they can qualify as Manager in their respective Divisions:

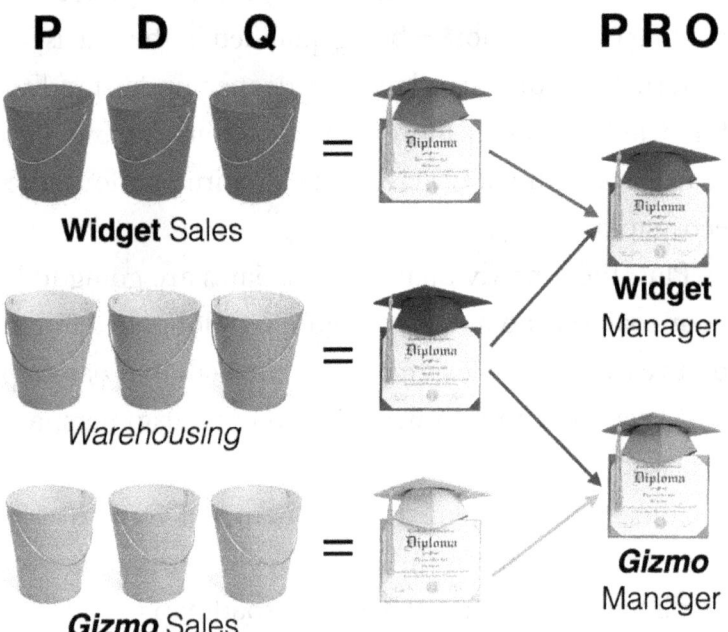

Besides the streamlined and modular advantage of stacking roadmaps, you can also use PDQ-Pro as a tool for regular review and polishing. A roadmap is just a plan that builds something systematically; in the case of your employees, it's knowledge, skill, judgement, and quality. Use it like a workout, but keep increasing the weights. Also, regular use will uncover changes or gaps in the references, procedures, and ecosystem. This will help you keep the roadmap updated and accurate.

Maybe the best way to think about PRQ-Pro integration is to visualize an upward spiral. The first time around gets you off the ground floor and climbing. Take it around again to build professionalism and prowess. Add more each time around the spiral. Eventually your new team member emerges as a professional manager and coach.

A professional is someone who never stops learning, never stops trying to get more and better-quality results. You have the tools now to make that happen!

PROFICIENCY - TAKEAWAYS
The PDQ-Pro process is the secret to spiral development.
Each time your team takes a new performer around the circle of Prepare, Develop, Qualify, Pro, they reinforce exactly what gets results and the whole team will prosper.

William Parry - Edward Beale

CHAPTER 14

THE SECRET SAUCE

The previous chapters unlocked the process to build a qualification roadmap *quickly*, with the people and stuff you already have. Now, here's the payoff. We're going to discuss why this is going to work, and why it'll work so well.

The roadmap is a shortcut to performance. It cuts out the side roads, distracting detours, and unproductive rest areas. You built the shortest route from unqualified to fully competent, and incorporated critical knowledge, skill, judgement, ecosystem integration, and quality metrics – all specific to the role and endorsed by your top performers.

Building competence is like painting a house. Adding enough coats mean the house is covered and looks great. PDQ-Pro gets the new hire "painted with competence" by high performing coaches and the roadmap. They do the **Prepare** homework with a "painter's" assist if needed. Then everyone works through the **Develop** section, adding a "coat of skill" with one painter, and another coat with the next. Eventually the "painting" is done, and you verify the job with **Qualify** checks. Is the house painted? Is it ready to be signed off? A couple touch-ups maybe, another swipe here or there. But yeah, we painted it together, it's DONE and looking great!

Here's another secret - your learners are "learning to learn" in this way. Your coaches are secretly learning to value the roadmap as a way to leverage what little time is available for training, and focus the conversation on only what is necessary to achieve results. Those details were selected by your seasoned cadré of experts, and the roadmap holds both learner and mentor accountable to the details of the performance.

Now that you have gone through this book, followed the examples, and built your first roadmap, you're set up for success. Your new hire has the opportunity to show off how motivated they are to learn the role quickly. Your established team has a clear trail along which to lead them, focused only on the few key things that get results. The entire team is working together, learning together, winning together.

You've spent nothing extra – no time away for 'training,' no expensive classes, no mismatch between the classroom and the workplace. Your people collaborate in real time to teach each other, adjust to real-world shifts in the ecosystem, and build trust and teamwork along the way. And it's all happening 'on the clock' as they continue to do quality work!

The next time a new performer joins the team you have a proven track for them to follow. What you want is for your new hire to become a coach for the *next* new hire, and show them the route. That's the secret sauce: the team begins to mentor and develop themselves.

Thanks for your efforts to **Prepare**, **Develop**, and **Qualify** the very best **Proficient** and **Professional** workforce, and (with a tight roadmap) do it *Pretty Darn Quick*.

We can't wait to hear all your stories of success!

- Bill & Ed

KEY TAKEAWAY
PDQ-Pro captures shortcuts to performance. Your people 'learn to learn' and develop themselves in a constant upward spiral of high performance and quality results.

PDQ-Pro Overview

	On your own	With your coach
Prepare *Fundamentals*	Study technical definitions Locate operational references Learn & review procedures	Review industry references Identify business contacts Schedule coaching sessions
Develop *Systems*	Begin any online development Practice operational processes Identify any problem areas	Build technical contact network Safety & efficiency techniques Build process speed & accuracy
Qualify *Activities*	Complete technical exams Complete sign-off process Pass oral & practical exams	Validate completed sign-offs Prepare candidate for exams Schedule oral & practical exams
Proficiency	Practice practice practice Stay up to date with what's new Become a coach for others	Transition from coach to colleague Build a professional network Help create new coaches

PROFESSIONAL NOTES

If you really enjoy the process of developing instruction and building human performance in a systematic way, read more about instructional design.

Throughout the book we use the terms *certification* and *qualification*. We know many sectors consider "certified" to mean an employee has gotten the green light to act with autonomy in the role. But we stuck with the military convention: certification refers to a location, system, or process; qualification refers to the performance of a human person. In short, you certify stuff, you qualify people. A facility can be certified even with no qualified people to run it. Likewise, an uncertified facility can still have perfectly qualified operators. Obviously, the best case is certified stuff and qualified people!

The quality check uses a method from instructional design, normally abbreviated PCS for 'performance, condition, standard.' Another well-known method is ABCD for Audience, Behavior, Condition, Degree. That might be great for academics. Just remember you are building a *rapid* set of qualification actions and checks. As you develop more and expanded roadmaps, you'll find what works for you. Focus on the role (audience) and write good performance objectives that include the "given" information and materials (condition(s)), the acceptable "watch me" action (performance(s)), and the level of quality (standard(s)), and you'll be fine.

Instructional designers often use a process known as ADDIE, which stands for Analyze, Design, Develop, Implement, and Evaluate. This is a specific case of Ed Beale's "ABCDE General Problem-Solving Model": Analyze, Blueprint, Construct, Deploy, Evaluate. Regardless of the model you pick, you still need to go through the same five steps: figure out where you are and what you have, create a plan of attack, build out a solution, implement it in the real world, and check how well you did. And then go back to the top and repeat the steps! Just like a good PDQ-Pro roadmap follows a spiral from **Preparation** to **Development** to **Qualification**, and (PROfessional) **PRO**ficiency, developing people starts somewhere and (hopefully) goes around the spiral in an upward and better direction.

Measurement leads to improvement. What gets measured gets repeated. Be sure you're measuring performances and behaviors that actually get results. Certainly, the scoreboard at the end is important (the *lag* measures). Just as important are your 'lead measures' – things that your team 1) can influence and 2) are predictive of success. Lead measures will get you results, guaranteed.

ACKNOWLEDGEMENTS

Bill would like to thank the Big Guy upstairs who set him on a path he did not know would lead to a life of amazing adventures. He would also like to thank his lifelong friend and partner in adventure, Ed Beale who helped guide him in developing this content, with the academic bumpers to his big picture ambitions. In addition, his wife Hilary (aka "the Pink Barracuda") who tolerated, pushed, cajoled and helped him along the way to complete this book. She has been the mortar to bricks of the foundation he has built.

Ed would like to thank his amazing wife Christine for encouragement, excellent editorial updates, and patient support. He also thanks his late wife Michelle who encouraged (and tolerated!) all the time away at conferences or writing this book. Of course, a hat tip to my author partner Bill Parry for sticking with this across a dozen years and a dozen moves – time to crack that bottle of Scotch!

They both thank their editor Alison (Downs) Petrowski for her exceptional work; any remaining errors are entirely the fault of the authors. They also would like to acknowledge their time as members of the U. S. Coast Guard, where they experienced military training methods and saw the benefit of adapting them for a wider corporate audience.

ABOUT THE AUTHORS

Bill Parry is a sales and revenue enablement leader with over 30 years of military and corporate experience, developing and delivering programs for companies of all sizes. His career began with the U.S. Coast Guard where he developed skills in leadership, instructional design, and human performance. In the corporate sales world, Bill quickly learned there was a huge disparity between content taught and what sellers did. Over the course of 25 plus years, Bill focused his energy building training and development programs that connected learning material with activities that produced real world results. This book is the culmination of that process.

Ed Beale is a retired U.S. Coast Guard officer, with service as a helicopter pilot, technical instructor, and academic dean of leadership development. He held private sector roles with GP Strategies, Metris Global, and Boston Scientific, and with nPlusOne brought PDQ-Pro to Trumpf North America, Arthur G. Russell, Bicron, and Stanley/Black & Decker. A Disney Institute graduate and speaker at learning, hacker, sales enablement, and leadership development events, Ed works to inspire positive corporate culture.

We'd love to help bring **PDQ-Pro** to your team.
Connect with us on LinkedIn.

www.ingramcontent.com/pod-product-compliance
Lightning Source LLC
Chambersburg PA
CBHW070503100426
42743CB00010B/1741